STUDY GUIDE AND SCORES FOR
THE UNDERSTANDING OF MUSIC
FIFTH EDITION

CHARLES R. HOFFER
University of Florida

Wadsworth Publishing Company
Belmont, California
A Division of Wadsworth, Inc.

Cover: *Rehearsal of the Pasdeloup Orchestra at the Cirque d'Hiver*
by John Singer Sargent. Courtesy, Museum of Fine Arts, Boston.

Printed in the United States of America

1 2 3 4 5 6 7 8 9 10---89 88 87 86 85

ISBN 0-534-03940-5

CONTENTS

LISTENING SCORES

PREFACE

This *Study Guide and Scores* is based on and coordinated with *The Understanding of Music*, Fifth Edition. The pages of the guide provide students with a self-instructional listening skills development program that supplements the "Listening Guides" in the textbook.

The review of information is provided by a Study Exercise for each of the thirty-five chapters in the textbook and three Composer Study Exercises. The pages use a variety of questions--matching, multiple-choice, true-false, completion, and short essay. A page reference with each question indicates the place in the textbook where the answer can be located.

The listening skills development program of fourteen practice pages asks students to respond on specific aspects of what they hear in the music--tempo, loudness, form, and so on. In a number of instances they are requested to compare works in different styles.

As is true of the parent textbook, the *Study Guide and Scores* allows for much flexibility in application. The pages are perforated for easy removal. Certain pages may be assigned as out-of-class work if desired, or the students may use them as an aid in reviewing. The pages may also be used for class discussions or testing. Flexibility is also aided by the separation of chapter study exercises, composer study exercises, and listening practice exercises.

Simplified scores and a libretto are included for eight of the works discussed in *The Understanding of Music*, Fifth Edition. The formal patterns of the musical works are indicated, most terms and foreign words translated, and the scores reduced to one or two staffs. These scores give the students something to follow while listening to the works, thereby helping them to keep their attention on the music and aiding them to understand the features of the music.

Charles R. Hoffer

Study Exercise 1

Music and Learning

1. Why should you learn more about music than you presently know?
   (p. 2)

2. What should you learn in a music appreciation course? (p. 3)

3. What is the greatest value of art music? (p. 4)
   a. to provide something interesting to listen to
   b. to offer the listener deep emotional release
   c. to provide pleasant diversion
   d. to promote group identity
   e. to lighten physical work

4. People should learn about art music because (p. 5)
   a. it is a mark of a "cultured" person
   b. it offers more reward in listening satisfaction
   c. it is better for social occasions
   d. it is simpler and easier to understand
   e. it is the music of mature persons

5. The type of music you know and the type of music you like are
   closely related. What implications does that statement have
   for students in a music course? (pp. 6-7)

   a. _____

   b. _____

   c. _____

Study Exercise 2

Listening to Music

1. Check the characteristics of the attitude needed to get the most out of listening to music. (11)

    _____ A feeling of complete contentment and relaxation

    _____ A willingness to put forth some effort

    _____ An awareness that you are dealing with something that is profound, subtle, and complex

    _____ Much interest in associating the music with specific nonmusical ideas

    _____ Much interest in what the composer does with sounds

    _____ A tolerance toward all types of music

2. What is the difference between listening for the music's sensuous qualities and listening for the music's expressive qualities? (9-10)

3. What does the word "listen" mean to a musician? (13)

4. Previous experiences in listening to popular music establish three expectations that are not helpful when listening to art music. The three factors are: (13)

    1. _____

    2. _____

    3. _____

5. Why is remembering so essential in listening to music? (12,14)

(continued)

6. A listener should attempt to become more sensitive to music and his or her reactions to it. (True or False)   (7-8)

7. Why shouldn't you attempt to visualize scenes as you listen?   (8)

Study Exercise 3

What Is Music? Melody and Harmony

1. Music can best be defined as: (22)
   a. something you enjoy listening to
   b. organized sounds
   c. something singable
   d. any sounds that are heard
   e. any sounds that have definite pitch

2. Why is it useful for a nonmusician student to know the basic terms for the various aspects of music? (22-23)

3. Match the word with the correct definition. (23)

   _____ a note eight notes away from the   Pitch
                       original

   _____ the degree of highness or lowness   Interval
                       of a sound

   _____ the distance between any two notes   Octave

4. What quality does a series of pitches need to be a melody? (23)

5. What makes the difference between a melody and a theme? (24)

6. What is the main difference between counterpoint and harmony, both of which involve the simultaneous sounding of pitches? (31)

(continued)

7. The basic structure of most chords is: (31)
   a.   every other pitch
   b.   two adjacent pitches and one a third away
   c.   three adjacent pitches
   d.   none of the above is correct

8. The word (consonance/dissonance) refers to an impression of tension
   in harmony.   (32)

9. The four voice parts in a standard arrangement for a choir of men
   and women are: (33)

   a.   _____

   b.   _____

   c.   _____

   d.   _____

Study Exercise 4

What Is Music? Rhythm, Loudness,
Timbre, and Form

1. The words "rhythm" and "beat" are synonymous.   (True or False)
    (35)

2. Meter refers to: (36)
    a.   the speed of the music
    b.   the flow of music in terms of time
    c.   the recurrent throb or pulse found in music
    d.   the pattern of beats
    e.   the pattern of notes

3. The composer can indicate the tempo of the music in two different
    ways.   (37-38)

    a.   _____

    b.   _____

4. Match the following terms.   (41)

    _____ Gradually get louder   Decrescendo

    _____ Gradually get softer   Crescendo

    _____ Tone quality   Loudness

    _____ Degree of loudness   Timbre
                     or softness

5. Timbre refers to: (41)
    a.   the speed of the music
    b.   the form of the music
    c.   tone qualities
    d.   loudness levels
    e.   the overall emotional effect of the music

6. Check the significant factors necessary for composing music.   (42-45)

    _____ Inspiration

    _____ Musical skills

    _____ Willingness to work at it

    _____ Nearly superhuman ability

(continued)

7. A song has four lines, the first two alike and the last two each different. How should the form be indicated? (44-45)
   a. *a a b b*
   b. *a a b c*
   c. *a b b c*
   d. *a a a b*
   e. *b b a c*

8. Check the elements that all pieces of music *must* possess. (Chapters 3 and 4)

   _____ Timbre   _____ Meter

   _____ Organization   _____ Rhythm

   _____ Pitch   _____ Loudness level

Listening Practice 1

Tempo

Determine the approximate speed of the music. Because words such as "fast" and "slow" are relative and depend somewhat on a person's individual definition, you may wish to listen to each selection once before marking your answer. Remember, listen to the speed of the beats, not the number of notes sounded.

	Slow	Moderate	Fast
1. Wagner--*Siegfried's Rhine Journey* (opening portion)			
2. Franck--Violin Sonata, fourth movement			
3. Handel--"For Unto Us" from *Messiah*			
4. Mozart--Piano Concerto No. 21, third movement			
5. Catten--Sonata for Flute, Oboe, Cello, & Harpsichord, first movement			
6. Bartok--Concerto for Orchestra, fifth movement			

Listen to the three works and rate them according to tempo. One way to help determine the tempo is to keep track of the number of beats in a fixed period of time, say 10 seconds. The slowest work can be marked with a "1" and the fastest with a "3."

Ranking

1. Berlioz—*Symphonie fantastique*, fourth movement

2. Hindemith—*Kleine Kammermusik*, Op. 24 No. 2, fifth movement

3. Haydn—String Quartet, Op. 76 No. 3, second movement

(Answers on page 85)

Musical Instruments: Orchestral and Band

1. Name the four instruments of the string family in addition to the harp. (46)

   a. _____   b. _____

   c. _____   d. _____

2. A vibrato is: (47)
   a. A rustling effect played by strings.
   b. A type of percussion instrument.
   c. The device on the oboe and bassoon that produces the sound.
   d. Rapid, small fluctuations of pitch.
   e. The simultaneous playing of two or more strings on a string instrument.

3. Match each woodwind instrument with the correct description. (49-52)

   _____ Low-pitched double-reed instrument   Flute

   _____ Does not have a reed   Clarinet

   _____ Has a single reed on a mouthpiece   Oboe

   _____ Higher-pitched double-reed   Bassoon
                    instrument

4. The saxophone comes in a variety of sizes. (True or False) (50)

5. Match each brass instrument with the correct descriptive fact. (51-52)

   _____ Has a slide   Trumpet

   _____ Highest-pitched brass instrument   French Horn

   _____ Largest and lowest-pitched brass   Trombone
                    instrument

   _____ Usually played with the hand   Tuba
                    inserted in the bell

6. Another name for timpani is _____. (53)

7. In what respect are the glockenspiel, xylophone, marimba, and vibraphone similar? (53)

(continued)

8. The piano belongs to the _____ family because its sounds
    are produced by a felt hammer striking a strong. (53)

9. What do the letters "Op." represent in the title of a musical
    composition? (56)

10. How does the instrumentation of the concert band differ from that of
     the orchestra? (57)

Study Exercise 6

Musical Instruments: Keyboard, Folk, and Popular

1. How does the harpsichord produce sounds?   (63-64)

2. What is the function of two of the pedals on a piano?   (65)

3. Check the statements that are true of the pipe organ.   (65-66)

    _____ Its keyboards are called manuals.

    _____ It has a pedalboard that is played with the feet.

    _____ It has 88 keys on each keyboard.

    _____ It has a set of pipes for each of its timbres.

    _____ By setting the knobs the organist can sound many notes when
    one key is depressed.

    _____ The best modern organs are designed to be very similar to
    the organs of Bach's time.

    _____ A pipe organ is an inexpensive instrument.

4. What are the differences between the traditional acoustic guitar
    and the electric guitar?   (68)

5. In what ways is an accordion similar to a small pipe organ?   (68-69)

(continued)

6. What are probably the most important "new" musical instruments?   (71)

7. How does the vocal mechanism operate to produce sounds?   (70-71)

Listening Practice 2

Meter

Determine which beats are accented, or stressed. The heavy beat is
the first in each pattern. Then indicate whether the pattern reveals a
beat grouping of two (or its multiple of four) or a grouping of three. It
may help to tap beats as you listen.

	Two- (or four-) beat meter	Three-beat meter
1. Brahms--Symphony No. 4, fourth movement		
2. Copland--"Simple Gifts"		
3. Britten--*The Young Person's Guide to the Orchestra*		
4. Mozart--Symphony No. 40, third movement		
5. Franck--Violin Sonata, fourth movement		

(Answers on page 85)

Musical Performance

1. Why is the performer's skill so important in rendering the music of
    the composer?   (74-75)

2. What are the advantages of a live performance over a recorded
    performance?   (75-78)

3. Musical notation is rather exact in only two respects. They are: (78,81)
    a. loudness and pitch
    b. pitch and rhythmic pattern
    c. loudness and rhythmic pattern
    d. expression and pitch
    e. rhythmic pattern and expression

4. The book containing all the parts in an instrumental composition is
    called the: (82)
    a. baton
    b. podium
    c. libretto
    d. score
    e. thesaurus

5. Why is a conductor needed for a musical group of much size?   (84)

6. What is the function of an arts council?   (87)

(continued)

7. What are the advantages and disadvantages of reviews of musical
    events?   (88-89)

8. Check the places when you applaud at a performance of instrumental
    music such as a symphony or string quartet.   (76-77)

    _____   When the conductor enters

    _____   At the conclusion of the first movement

    _____   At the conclusion of the entire work

    _____   Just after a soloist has played a passage especially well

9. What information is usually contained in the printed concert
    program?   (75,77)

Folk and Ethnic Music

1. "Folk" and "ethnic" are synonymous. (True or False) (92)

2. How is most folk-ethnic music created? (93)

3. How does much of the world's folk-ethnic music differ from Western
    art music in terms of: (94-97)
    a. Rhythm:

    b. Harmony:

    c. Improvisation:

4. A microtone is: (95)
    a. a very short note
    b. a pitch that is less than a half step from another pitch
    c. a note that is played but not written in notation
    d. a note that is played for a shorter time than the notation
        indicates
    e. a type of ornamented note found in Indian music

5. Modes are: (96)
    a. the feelings one gets from a piece of music
    b. the style of singing used in various types of music
    c. the choice of instrumental ensemble used for folk music
    d. non-major/minor seven-note scale patterns
    e. scales containing five notes

(continued)

Study Exercise 10

Renaissance Music

1. What are the approximate dates of the Renaissance period in music? (124)

2. A good example of the "Renaissance man" is: (128)
    a. Thomas Aquinas
    b. Pope Gregory I
    c. Leonardo da Vinci
    d. Martin Luther
    e. Pythagoras

3. Check those characteristics that apply to the Renaissance motet and those that apply to the madrigal.   (132-138)

	Motet	Madrigal
In vernacular language		
In Latin		
Sometimes contains a phrase from Gregorian chant		
Much melodic imitation		
Some melodic imitation		

4. Fill in the names of three English, three Netherlandian, three French, three German, three Italian, and two Spanish Renaissance composers.   (140-142)

    English _____

    Netherlandian _____

    French _____

German _____

Italian _____

Spanish _____

Listening Practice 4

Presence of Regular Metrical Patterns

Determine whether the music has a regular or irregular metrical pattern.

	Regular beat pattern	Irregular beat pattern
1. Bernstein—"The Dance at the Gym" from *West Side Story*		
2. Franck—Violin Sonata, fourth movement		
3. Hindemith—*Kleine Kammermusik,* Op. 24 No. 2, fifth movement		
4. Handel—"Every Valley Shall Be Exhalted" from *Messiah*		
5. Gershwin—"Bess, You Is My Woman Now" from *Porgy and Bess*		
6. Crumb—*Night of the Four Moons*		

(Answers on page 85)

Study Exercise 11

Baroque Vocal Music: Recitative and Aria

1. Check the items that are characteristic of the Baroque period. (143-146)

   _____ A fondness for the large and grandiose

   _____ Reason and restraint

   _____ Intense religious feeling

   _____ A love of the dramatic

   _____ An interest in mechanical objects

   _____ A strong other-worldly outlook

2. Check the statements that are true of recitatives. (148,150-152)

   _____ Sung in strict rhythm

   _____ Frequently repeat words

   _____ Complex, "thick" accompaniment

   _____ Usually four or more minutes long

   _____ Often very expressive

3. What is homophony? (150-151)

4. A series of two or three chords used to indicate the end of a musical phrase is called a: (152)
   a. modulation
   b. mode
   c. cadence
   d. choral setting
   e. tonic

5. The process of changing key is called: (152)
   a. modulation
   b. mode
   c. cadence
   d. choral setting
   e. tonic

(continued)

6. List five features of an aria.   (152-157)

   a. _____

   b. _____

   c. _____

   d. _____

   e. _____

7. Music that demonstrates a performer's ability in a showy way is called
   _____ music.   (155)

Study Exercise 12

Baroque Vocal Music: Oratorio and Cantata

1. An oratorio: (160)
    a. has no staging, costumes, or actions
    b. uses a chorus, soloists, and orchestra
    c. usually has a religious theme
    d. is not conceived for presentation in a worship service
    e. all of the above are true

2. A chorus part in an oratorio is more like a (recitative/aria) than
    a (recitative/aria).   (161)

3. The chorus in an oratorio is often: (161)
    a. contrapuntal, polyphonic
    b. unaccompanied
    c. slow
    d. for one or two performers
    e. without meter

4. The Protestant hymn developed in the Reformation is: (165-166)
    a. solid, serious, and uncluttered
    b. a type of chant
    c. called a chorale
    d. highly dramatic
    e. true of (a) and (c), but not (b) and (d)

5. What is the main difference between an oratorio and a cantata?   (166)

6. The doctrine of affections was: (168)
    a. a belief in free love
    b. a belief in the state of mind projected by the music
    c. an international agreement whereby composers could use each
        other's themes
    d. an edict from the Pope forbidding bawdy songs
    e. a book of explicit love-making songs published in 1694

(continued)

7. Match the correct term with the descriptive phrase.   (137,171)

_____ A religious Renaissance choral work   Requiem

_____ A nonreligious Renaissance choral   Motet
                    work

_____ An oratorio on the story of the   Madrigal
                    Crucifixion

Baroque Instrumental Music: The Fugue

1. An adaptation of a piece of music written for an instrument or voice
    to another instrument or voice, or to a group of either is called:
    (174)
    a. a harmonization
    b. an orchestration
    c. an affectation
    d. a transcription
    e. a duet

2. Check the instruments that were especially significant during the
    Baroque period. (174-175)

    _____ Organ   _____ Harpsichord

    _____ Trumpet   _____ Clarinet

    _____ Piano   _____ Percussion

    _____ Guitar   _____ Flute

3. What was the tuning problem that was finally worked out in the
    Baroque period? (176)

4. During the Baroque period abrupt changes from loud to soft were the
    rule, and not the gradual changes we are accustomed to today. These
    abrupt changes are called: (176-177)
    a. crescendos
    b. terraced dynamics
    c. *basso continuo*
    d. unequal temperament
    e. dynamic progressions

5. What is the *continuo* in Baroque music? (172)

(continued)

6. Sketch the diagram for a three-voice fugue, with the subject opening in the middle voice. (183)

7. A sequence results when a melodic figure is repeated several times in succession: (183)
   a. each time at a different pitch level
   b. each time at the same pitch level
   c. each time with a different rhythmic pattern
   d. each time with one pitch changed
   e. each time with the rhythm changed somewhat

8. Match the type of keyboard music in the right-hand column with the description in the left-hand column. (182-187)

   _____ A short piece of instrumental music   Chorale variations

   _____ A contrapuntal work build on a theme called a "subject"   Passacaglia

   _____ Continuous variations on a theme in the bass   Prelude

   _____ Variations on a hymnlike theme   Toccata

   _____ A flashy virtuoso work, usually for keyboard instrument   Fugue

9. "Pedal point" in a work of music is a place where: (186)
   a. all the performers are sounding the same pitch
   b. a low instrument such as a cello plays a note higher than a high instrument such as the violin
   c. a rhythmic pattern is repeated persistently
   d. one long tone is maintained against changing harmonies in the other parts
   e. a sequence is terminated

Study Exercise 14

Baroque Instrumental Music: The Suite and Concerto Grosso

1. What are the differences between dance music for dancing and dance music that has been stylized for listening?   (188)

2. The usual four dances in a suite composed during Bach's lifetime are: (188-189)
   a. minuet, waltz, gigue, bourrée
   b. allemande, courante, sarabande, gigue
   c. allemande, minuet, courante, gigue
   d. bourrée, minuet, allemande, courante
   e. sarabande, waltz, bourrée, gigue

3. During the Baroque period the word "sonata" referred to a work: (193)
   a. that is polyphonic
   b. played on untuned instruments
   c. of instrumental music
   d. in a certain form
   e. for two or more instruments

4. The basic principle of all concertos is: (193)
   a. a virtuoso solo part
   b. a contrast of groups of different sizes or instrumentation
   c. sonata form
   d. triple meter
   e. none of the above are true

5. Check the statements that are true of a Baroque concerto grosso: (193-194)

   _____ It utilizes a small group of soloists.

   _____ The soloists' part is much more flashy than the music for the large group.

   _____ Usually it is for strings and harpsichord.

   _____ Often it uses a chorale melody as a theme.

   _____ It is based on the idea of contrast between groups of instruments.

Baroque Composers Study Exercise

Match each of the following composers with the correct description
of his musical achievements.

Giovanni Gabrieli   Arcangelo Corelli
Claudio Monteverdi   Antonio Vivaldi
Heinrich Schütz   Georg Phillipp Telemann
Jean-Baptiste Lully   Johann Sebastian Bach
Henry Purcell   George F. Handel

1. _____ Very innovative; began in Renaissance
                                    style; wrote some of the early successful
                                    operas

2. _____ Wrote Italian operas in England; very
                                    important oratorio composer

3. _____ Composer to King of France; staged ballets;
                                    developed French overture

4. _____ German who composed over 3,000 works of all
                                    types

5. _____ Forecast Baroque musical style; put choirs
                                    on each side of St. Mark's in Venice

6. _____ Greatest German composer of Baroque;
                                    especially known for organ and religious
                                    music

7. _____ English composer; successful in many types
                                    of music

8. _____ Italian composer who contributed to violin
                                    and orchestral music

9. _____ Italian who composed great amount of fine
                                    music, including concertos for bassoon,
                                  piccolo, and guitar; former priest

Renaissance and Baroque Compared

Compare Palestrina's *Sicut Cervus* with the "For Unto Us a Child Is Born" from *Messiah* by Handel. Because many aspects of music are not "either-or" in nature, most of the items are set on a line to represent a continuum. You can put "S" on the line for your response on the *Sicut Cervus* and "F" for your response on the "For Unto Us a Child Is Born."

1. Size of performing group

    Solo or small group _____ Large group

2. Melody

    Melodies not prominent _____ Melodies very prominent

    Narrow pitch range _____ Wide pitch range

    Smooth, songlike, continuously flowing _____ Short and fragmented

    No repeated patterns _____ Many repeated patterns

    Plain and unadorned _____ Highly ornamented

3. Rhythm

    Beat very prominent _____ Beat subtle or nonexistent

    Rigid tempo _____ Flexible tempo

    Regular metrical pattern _____ Irregular metrical pattern

    Simple rhythmic structure _____ Complex rhythmic structure

4. Harmony

    Contrapuntal-   Some sections contra-
      polyphonic   puntal; some homophonic   Homophonic

5. Loudness

    Generally soft _____ Generally loud

    Few changes of loudness level ____ Many changes of loudness level

    Sudden, abrupt loudness changes   Smooth, gradual loudness changes

6. Timbre

    Consistent _____ Many wide changes

7. Form

    Short _____ Long

    Little repetition of material ____ Much repetition of material

Classicism, Classical Music, and Sonata Form

1. The Rococo is especially associated with the sumptuous court of the
    King of: (200)
    a.   France
    b.   England
    c.   Russia
    d.   Italy
    e.   Germany (Prussia)

2. What are the approximate dates of the Classical period in music?
    (201)

3. Check the features of the intellectual outlook of the Classical
    period.   (201-204)

    _____ Love of nature

    _____ Belief in the process of reason

    _____ Belief in the universal nature of truth

    _____ Trust in emotions

    _____ Fondness of mystery

4. The system under which a composer accepted exclusive employment under
    one wealthy person or family was called: (201)
    a.   serfdom
    b.   patronage
    c.   parentalism
    d.   indentured status
    e.   artist-in-residence

5. The first theme in the first movement of Mozart's Symphony No. 40 is
    typical in that it is a continuous, arching flow of notes spanning
    eight measures.   (True or False)   (207)

6. In sonata form the second theme is (similar to/different from) the
    first theme and in the (same/different) key.   (208)

(continued)

7. Draw and label the pattern (schema) for sonata form. (212)

The Classical Symphony and Concerto

1. The symphony and symphony orchestra had its founding in: (214)
    a.   Berlin
    b.   Vienna
    c.   Mannheim
    d.   Paris
    e.   Salzburg

2. Check the features of the typical second movement of a symphony. (214)

    _____ Slow tempo

    _____ Much development of themes

    _____ Longest movement

    _____ Melodious

    _____ Virtuoso music

3. The word *sforzando* means: (215)
    a.   a sudden stop
    b.   a hold in the music
    c.   a short melodic or rhythmic pattern that acts as a unifying
         element in the music
    d.   a short ornamental note
    e.   a sudden accent or loud note

4. A "motive" in music is: (215)
    a.   the motivation that caused the composer to write the work
    b.   the playing of the theme in a key different from the original
    c.   a short melodic or rhythmic pattern that acts as a unifying
         element in the music
    d.   a theme that is used in more than one movement of a work
    e.   an ornamental figure involving five notes in a specified pattern

5. Draw and label the pattern (schema) of a symphonic movement that is
    a minuet and trio.   (218)

6. Check the characteristics that make a concerto different from a
    symphony.   (Entire chapter)

    _____ A concerto often has three movements.

    _____ A concerto often has a double exposition in sonata form.

    (continued)

_____ A concerto involves an orchestra.

_____ A concerto has a part for a soloist or small group.

_____ A concerto often has a melodious second movement.

7. A cadenza is: (223)
   a. a repeated pattern played by drums
   b. the final two chords in a phrase
   c. a special type of concerto
   d. a free solo section in a concerto
   e. the stick held by the conductor

8. Check the patterns that are rondos. (224)

   _____ A B A   _____ A B B A C C

   _____ A B A B   _____ A B A C A B A

   _____ A B A C A   _____ A B C A D

   _____ A B A B C A

9. Compare the music of the Classical period with that of the Baroque period by checking the characteristics that are true for each period. (226-227)

	Baroque	Classical
Homophonic texture predominate		
Basso continuo		
Terraced dynamics		
Melodies composed of short ideas strung together		
Organ and harpsichord important instruments		
Solo concerto		
Metrical rhythm		
Sonata form		
Modulation to nearly related keys		

Listening Practice 6

Melodic Contour

A melody can be smooth in contour with most of its notes moving to
neighboring steps, as in "America" ("My Country, 'Tis of Thee"). Or a
melody can contain many skips to distant notes, as in "The Star-Spangled
Banner." Of the melodies listed below, decide which ones move generally
from one note to a neighboring note and which ones frequently jump to
distant pitches. Don't let your judgment be confused by the style of playing or singing; consider only the contour of the melody.

	Moves to adjacent notes	Contains many skips to notes not adjacent
1. Franck--Violin Sonata, fourth movement		
2. Morley--"April Is in My Mistress' Face"		
3. Bach--Fugue in C Major		
4. Schoenberg--Variations for Orchestra		
5. Ives--"Serenity"		
6. Mendelssohn--Symphony No. 4, first movement		

(Answers on page 85)

Melodic Style

Determine whether the music is performed in a smooth manner or in a separated style. The contour of the melody should not be considered in this case.

	Smooth	Separated
1. Gershwin--"Bess, You Is My Woman Now" from *Porgy and Bess*		
2. Mozart--Piano Concerto, No. 21 first movement		
3. Hindemith--*Kleine Kammermusik*, Op. 24 No. 2, fifth movement		
4. Mussorgsky--Boris Godunov, "Coronation Scene" (opening section)		
5. Bach--Cantata No. 140, part IV		
6. Villa-Lobos--*Bachianas Brasileiras No. 5*, "Aria"		

(Answers on page 85)

Study Exercise 17

Classical Opera

1. Opera is a unification of a number of art forms. How is this fact
    both an advantage and a disadvantage? (228-230)

2. What are some operatic conventions that one accept in order to
    enjoy opera? (228-230)

3. Opera began shortly before 1600 in Florence, Italy, as an attempt to:
    (234)
    a. protest against the Council of Trent's guidelines for church
        music
    b. supplement stage plays
    c. revive the authentic form of ancient Greek dramas
    d. find a new style of church music
    e. add instrumental accompaniments to motets

4. The first operas drew upon stories and characters from the Old
    Testament. (True or False) (234)

5. The text of an opera is called the: (232)
    a. verse
    b. parlance
    c. parlando
    d. libretto
    e. buffa

6. Mozart's *The Marriage of Figaro* is made up of arias, recitatives,
    and ensemble music. (True or False). (233-238)

Chamber Music

1. Define the term "chamber music." (238-239)

2. List four ways in which a composer can vary a theme. (249)

    a. _____

    b. _____

    c. _____

    d. _____

3. In the Classical period the sonata took on a more precise meaning.
    What are the two types of Classical sonatas? (244)

4. Check the statements that are true of the sonata since the time of
    Mozart and Haydn. (244)

    _____ It is for piano and two other instruments.

    _____ The piano is not for accompaniment but rather is an equal
           member.

    _____ It has only one movement.

    _____ It often utilizes sonata form.

    _____ It is usually played from memory.

5. What instruments make up a string quartet? (244)

(continued)

6. What instruments make up a woodwind quintet? (250)

7. A piano trio is made up of: (250)
    a. piano, violin, and cello
    b. piano, violin, and viola
    c. three pianos
    d. piano, trumpet, and French horn
    e. none of the above

Listening Practice 7

Baroque and Classical Compared

Compare Corelli's *Christmas Concerto* with Mozart's Symphony No. 40, first movement. Because many aspects of music are not "either-or" in nature, most of the items are set on a line to represent a continuum. You can put "C" on the line for your response on the concerto grosso of Corelli and "M" for your response on the Mozart symphony.

1. Size of performing group

   Solo or small group _____ Large group

2. Melody

   Melodies not prominent _____ Melodies very prominent

   Narrow pitch range _____ Wide pitch range

   Smooth songlike, continuously flowing ___ Short and fragmented

   No repeated patterns _____ Many repeated patterns

   Plain and unadorned _____ Highly ornamented

3. Rhythm

   Beat very prominent _____ Beat subtle or nonexistent

   Simple rhythmic structure _____ Complex rhythmic structure

4. Harmony

   Contrapuntal-   Some sections contra-
     polyphonic   puntal; some homophonic   Homophonic

   Centers strongly on one key _____ In no key

   Generally major   Generally minor   Other

5. Loudness

   Generally soft _____ Generally loud

   Few changes of loudness level ___ Many changes of loudness level

6. Timbre

   Consistent _____ Many wide changes

7. Form

   Short _____ Long

   Little repetition of material ___ Much repetition of material

42

Study Exercise 19

Beethoven: From Classicism to Romanticism

1. Check the statements that are true about Beethoven's *Pathétique* Sonata. (259-263)

   _____ It has a slow, brooding introduction.

   _____ It is the last piano sonata Beethoven composed.

   _____ It is in the style of Mozart's and Haydn's piano sonatas.

   _____ The first movement is in sonata form.

   _____ It contains many *sforzandi*.

   _____ The third movement is in sonata form.

   _____ It exploits the possible range and powerful sounds of the piano.

2. In many first movements Beethoven used sonata form. However, he expanded one portion of it. What portion was increased in importance? (267)

3. Beethoven's melodies are nearly always rough and masculine. (True or False) (268)

4. Check the main features of the minuet of Mozart's symphonies and the scherzo as found in Beethoven's symphonies. (217-218 and 269)

	Minuet	Scherzo	Both	Neither
Fast tempo				
Triple meter				
ABA form				
Eighteenth-century dance				
Development section				

(continued)

5. When a theme appears in more than one movement of a work, the term
    for this technique is: (271)
    a. canon
    b. development
    c. contrapuntal
    d. cyclical
    e. transposition

6. More than any composer before him (and probably also since) Beethoven
    was able to: (Entire chapter)
    a. develop themes
    b. write counterpoint
    c. create new forms
    d. exploit the sonorities of orchestral instruments
    e. inject nonmusical associations ("victory," "love," and so on)
          into instrumental music

7. *Egmont*, for which Beethoven wrote music, was: (271-273)
    a. an opera
    b. a ballet
    c. a drama
    d. a coronation of a king
    e. nothing; it was a name Beethoven gave this work

8. Check the statements that are true about Beethoven's music.
    (Entire chapter)

    _____ It bridges the Baroque and Classical styles.

    _____ It sometimes contains a long build-up to a climactic point.

    _____ It follows the doctrine of affections by maintaining a con-
            sistent mood throughout a movement.

    _____ It almost never follows established forms such as a sonata,
            rondo, and the like.

    _____ It contains many abrupt changes of loudness level.

    _____ It contains only a limited amount of thematic development.

    _____ It sounds a great deal like Mozart's and Haydn's later works.

    _____ Almost all melodies in it are very singable.

Major/Minor

Most music in Western civilization is in either a major or minor key. This does not mean that all chords in a major key are major chords. Rather, it means that the harmonies are arranged in such a way that their progression suggests a strong feeling of major or minor tonality. Some works are in neither a major nor a minor key. If there is no feeling of key center, as in one of the excerpts listed below, the music is without tonality. Determine the tonality of each excerpt.

	Major	Minor	No key
1. Borodin—*Nocturne*			
2. Mozart--Piano Concerto No. 21, third movement			
3. Brahms—Symphony No. 4, fourth movement			
4. Schoenberg—Variations for Orchestra			
5. Prokofiev--Violin Concerto No. 2, first movement			
6. Handel--"For Unto Us a Child Is Born" from *Messiah*			
7. Schubert--"The Erl King"			

(Answers on page 85)

Study Exercise 20

Early Romantic Music: Songs and Choral Music

1. Check the characteristics that are true of the Romantic attitude. (276-280)

   _____ Trusts one's feelings

   _____ Admires reason and intellect

   _____ Preoccupied with the here-and-now

   _____ Enjoys struggle against great or even hopeless odds

   _____ Loves nature

   _____ Resents rules and restraints

   _____ Feels that works of art are personal creations

   _____ Artists and composers are often nonsocial or antisocial

2. What about the Faust legend probably attracted Romantic writers and composers? (279)

3. The composer of an art song also was usually the writer of the words for the song. (True or False) (282)

4. Check the statements that are true of art songs. (282-287)

   _____ The piano part is very important.

   _____ Many are through-composed.

   _____ Some are strophic.

   _____ They are often called *lieder*.

   _____ They seek to show off the singer's vocal technique.

   _____ They seek to achieve maximum expression of the text.

5. A song in which the stanzas of a poem are set to basically the same music is called _____. (284)

6. Some composers continued to write oratorios in the Romantic period. (True or False) (289)

Early Romantic Music: Piano Music

1. A "character piece" is" (292-293)
   a. a work by an eccentric composer
   b. a special type of piano sonata
   c. a set of stylized Polish dances
   d. a short free-sounding piano work composed in the nineteenth-century
   e. an art song with an extensive part for the piano

2. Which work is *not* a title of a nineteenth-century character piece for piano? (293)
   a. fantasie
   b. ballade
   c. sonata
   d. impromptu
   e. etude

3. The term rubato means: (293)
   a. "rolling" a chord
   b. slight rhythmic deviations from the printed music
   c. leaving out the pedal at places where it is indicated
   d. playing piano work on the grand piano
   e. omitting some of the indicated ornamentation in the melody

4. A consonant note in a chord that is held over into the next chord, where it is a dissonant note, and then moves down a step to a consonant note is called: (295)
   a. transmutation
   b. progression
   c. suspension
   d. inversion
   e. diversion

5. Liszt's *La Campanella* contains much: (301-304)
   a. virtuoso piano writing
   b. contrapuntal writing
   c. development of themes
   d. danceable music
   e. music in the style of Handel and Bach

(continued)

6. Compare the music of the Romantic period with that of the Classical period by checking the characteristics that are true for each period. (306)

	Classical	Romantic
Art song developed		
Broad, flowing melodies		
Few public concerts		
Modulations to many keys		
Very steady beat		
Undulating dynamics		
Careful use of formal patterns		
Rich harmonies		
Virtuoso piano music		

Listening Practice 9

Changes of Timbre

Determine whether or not the timbre changes significantly during the music.

	Much change	Little or no change
1. Britten—*The Young Person's Guide to the Orchestra*		
2. Copland—*Appalachian Spring* (excerpt)		
3. G. Gabrieli—"Canzona per Sonare No. 4"		
4. Berlioz—*Symphonie fantasique*, fourth movement		
5. Haydn—String Quartet, Op. 76 No. 3, second movement		
6. Crumb—*Night of the Four Moons*		
7. Liszt—*La Campanella*		

(Answers on page 85)

Program Music and Ballet

1. Define the term "program music." (307)

2. Music without any nonmusical associations is called: (307)
    a. nonrepresentational
    b. absolute
    c. abstract
    d. neuter
    e. nonassociative

3. To listen intelligently to a work of program music, you must know the nonmusical association of the music. (True or False) (307)

4. Match the type of program music in the right-hand column with the description in the left-hand column. (308)

    _____ A programmatic overture   Symphonic poem

    _____ Instrumental works often   Concert overture
                       associated with a drama

    _____ Another name for symphonic   Tone poem
                       poem

    _____ A long, complex, programmatic   Incidental music
                       work for orchestra

5. How does theme transformation differ from theme development and theme variation? (310)

6. Richard Strauss' *Don Juan* is loosely in: (316)
    a. three-part form
    b. rondo form
    c. theme-and-variation form
    d. sonata form
    e. passacaglia form

(continued)

7. The designer of the dances for a ballet is called the: (319)
   a. chorus master
   b. conductor de ballet
   c. choreographer
   d. impresario
   e. concertmaster

8. When an orchestra plays *Swan Lake* in a concert, the music is not the complete ballet, but rather a suite arranged by the composer himself. (True or False)   (324)

Study Exercise 23

Romantic Opera

1. The term *bel canto* refers to a style of opera that emphasized
    _____. (327)

2. As opera progressed through the nineteenth century, especially in the
    operas of Verdi and Wagner, the distinction between recitative and
    aria became (less/greater). (327, 336)

3. What are the differences between Wagner's music drama and the more
    typical operas of his time? (336-337)

4. Wagner frequently associates a melodic fragment with a person or
    idea. Such a fragment is called: (336)
    a. a theme
    b. a personification
    c. a *leitmotiv*
    d. an *idee fixe*
    e. a rubato

Listening Practice 10

Melodic Phrases

Some melodies seem to be a continuous string of notes. Other melodies consist of short phrases that have been combined to form a longer unit. In this practice exercise, determine which type of melody is heard in each example.

	Combination of short melodic phrases	Continuous melodic line
1. Villa-Lobos—*Bachianas Brasileiras No. 5*, "Aria"		
2. Mozart—Symphony No. 40, first movement		
3. Puccini—*La Bohème*, Act I		
4. Mozart—*The Marriage of Figaro*, "Se voul ballace"		
5. Hindemith—*Kleine Kammermusik*, Op. 24 No. 2, fifth movement		

(Answers on page 85)

1. What happens to the note values of a theme when it is played in diminution? (346)

2. What happens to the note values of a theme when it is played in augmentation? (346)

3. Check the things Brahms does with themes. (346-348)

    _____ Presents them in augmentation

    _____ Presents them in diminution

    _____ Fragments them

    _____ Exchanges fragments of them among instruments

    _____ Transforms them

    _____ Uses them in sonata form

    _____ Writes variations on them

4. What are the characteristics of a passacaglia-chaconne? (350)

5. A canon is most similar to a: (353)
    a. sonata
    b. round
    c. variation
    d. recitative
    e. strophic song

(continued)

6. Dvořák wrote his Cello Concerto in Spillville, Iowa. Therefore, it is American music.   (True or False)   (356)

7. What is unusual about the sonata form in the first movement of Dvořák's Cello Concerto?   (357)

Classical and Romantic Compared

Compare the fourth movement of Berlioz's *Symphonie fantastique* with the third movement of Mozarts' Piano Concerto No. 21. You can put an "M" on the line for your response on Mozarts' music and an "B" for Berlioz's music.

1. Size of performing group

    Solo or small group   Large group

2. Melody

    Melodies not prominent   Melodies very prominent

    Smooth, songlike, continuously flowing   Short and fragmented

    No repeated patterns   Many repeated patterns

    Plain and unadorned   Highly ornamented

                                                    Functions as theme; is
    No development or variation   developed and varied

3. Rhythm

    Beat very prominent   Beat subtle or nonexistent

    Rigid tempo   Flexible tempo

    Regular metrical pattern   Many changes in metrical pattern

4. Harmony

    Contrapuntal-   Some sections contra-
      polyphonic   puntal; some homophonic   Homophonic

    Basic chords predominant   Rich harmonic structure

    Generally consonant chords   Many dissonant chords

5. Loudness

    Few changes of loudness level   Many changes of loudness level

    Sudden, abrupt loudness changes   Smooth, gradual loudness changes

6. Timbre

    Consistent   Many wide changes

7. Form

    Short   Long

    Little repetition of material   Much repetition of material

Study Exercise 25

Nationalism

1. How does nationalism make its presence felt in music?   (359-360)

2. Which of these Russian composers is generally *not* considered as being nationalistic?   (361)
   a. Tchaikovsky
   b. Mussorgsky
   c. Rimsky-Korsakov
   d. Borodin
   e. Glinka

3. A whole-tone scale contains no half steps. (True or False)   (364)

4. Check the musical factors that are found in Mussorgsky's *Boris Godunov*.   (361-366)

   _____ Polymeters

   _____ Russian folksongs

   _____ Basso continuo

   _____ Whole tone scales

   _____ Use of modulations to distant keys

   _____ Two orchestras; one in front of the stage and another on it

   _____ Interlude for the ringing of bells

5. What three composers are most associated with nineteenth-century Hungarian-Bohemian nationalism?   (367)

   a. _____

   b. _____

   c. _____

6. Match the composer with his native land.   (367-371)

   _____ England   Jean Sibelius

   _____ Italy   Edward Elgar

   _____ Finland   Ottorino Respighi

   _____ Spain   Bedřich Smetana

   _____ Hungary-Bohemia   Manuel de Falla

Study Exercise 26

Impressionism and Post-Romanticism

1. Impressionism is largely associated with: (372)
   a. Germany
   b. Hungary
   c. England
   d. Spain
   e. France

2. What are the basic artistic beliefs of impressionism?   (372-373)

3. As is true of no other artistic style, impressionism represents a consistent point of view among poets, painters, and musicians. (True or False)   (373)

4. Check the characteristics that are true of impressionistic music. (375-378)

   _____ Decisive and clear-cut rhythmic patterns

   _____ Strict tempo

   _____ Strong melodic structure

   _____ Rich harmonies

   _____ Much development of themes

   _____ Attention to special tone qualities of instruments

   _____ Free treatment of dissonance

5. Who are three prominent Post-Romantic composers?   (379-381)

   a. _____

   b. _____

   c. _____

Listening Practice 12

Impressionistic and Romantic Music Compared

Compare Debussy's *Prelude to the Afternoon of a Faun* with Liszt's *La Campanella*. You can put a "D" on the line for your response on Debussy's music and an "L" for Liszt's music.

1. Size of performing group

   Solo or small group _____ Large group

2. Melody

   Melodies not prominent _____ Melodies very prominent

   Smooth, songlike, continuously flowing _____ Short and fragmented

   No repeated patterns _____ Many repeated patterns

   Plain and unadorned _____ Highly ornamented

3. Rhythm

   Beat very prominent _____ Beat subtle or nonexistent

   Rigid tempo _____ Flexible tempo

   Simple rhythmic structure _____ Complex rhythmic structure

4. Harmony

   Contrapuntal-   Some sections contra-
     polyphonic   puntal; some homophonic   Homophonic

   Basic chords predominant _____ Rich harmonic structure

   Generally consonant chords _____ Many dissonant chords

5. Loudness

   Generally soft _____ Generally loud

   Few changes of loudness level _____ Many changes of loudness level

   Sudden, abrupt loudness changes _____ Smooth, gradual loudness changes

6. Form

   Short _____ Long

   Little repetition of material _____ Much repetition of material

   A B A _____ Theme and variations

Romantic Composers Study Exercise

Ludwig van Beethoven   Franz Liszt   Jean Sibelius
Hector Berlioz   Sergei Rachmaninoff   Richard Strauss
Johannes Brahms   Giacomo Puccini   Peter Tchaikovsky
Frederic Chopin   Franz Schubert   Giuseppi Verdi
Antonin Dvorak   Robert Schumann   Richard Wagner

1. _____ French composer; skillful in writing for instruments; imaginative programmatic music.

2. _____ Russian composer of symphonies, operas, and ballet music; not very nationalistic.

3. _____ Leader in early nineteenth-century music; German composer of piano music, symphonies, and chamber works; edited a magazine.

4. _____ Great German opera composer; called his operas "music dramas"; wrote his own librettos.

5. _____ Polish composer of piano music who spent much of his life in France; close friend of George Sand.

6. _____ Post romantic Russian composer of symphonies and piano works; songlike melodies.

7. _____ Finland's greatest composer; wrote symphonies and concertos, plus some programmatic music.

8. _____ Italian opera composer; wrote *La Boheme* and *Madame Butterfly*.

9. _____ Outstanding conservative German composer of symphonies, concertos, and chamber works, but wrote no operas.

10. _____ Outstanding Italian opera composer and patriot; composed *Aida* and *La Traviata*.

11. _____ Great German-Austrian composer; began writing in Classical period but evolved into Romantic; fiery symphonies, overtures, and piano music.

12. _____ Early Austrian composer and virtuoso pianist; wrote much piano music and tone poems; influenced by Paganini.

(continued)

13. _____ Austrian composer; versatile but best known for his hundreds of art songs.

14. _____ German composer of tone poems and operas; lived well into the twentieth century.

15. _____ Hungarian-Bohemian composer who wrote some of his best works while living in the United States.

Twentieth-Century Music: Mainstream Instrumental

1. What are some of the factors in the twentieth century that have affected the viewpoints and attitudes of composers?   (386-387)

2. The rhythm of twentieth-century music is marked by: (387, 390)
    a.   polyrhythms
    b.   mixed meters
    c.   polymeters
    d.   increased use of percussion
    e.   all of the above

3. In what way do melodies in twentieth-century music differ from those of preceding centuries?   (390-391)

4. Harmony in twentieth-century music sometimes contains: (391-392)
    a.   polychords
    b.   no tonal center
    c.   chords in fourths
    d.   nontraditional chords progressions
    e.   all of the above

5. Both harmony and counterpoint in twentieth-century music contain an increased amount of _____.   (392-393)

6. What has happened to the size of the orchestra specified for many twentieth-century works?   (393)

7. Twentieth-century composers have been more interested in timbres, including unconventional ones, than their predecessors.   (True or False)   (393)

(continued)

8. The first movement of Prokofiev's Violin Concerto No. 2 is in
   _____ form. (403)

Study Exercise 28

Twentieth-Century Music: Mainstream Vocal

1. Check the aspects of pretwentieth-century music found in Britten's
    A Ceremony of Carols. (407-409)

    _____ Chant-like melodies

    _____ Latin and old English texts

    _____ Points of imitation

    _____ Canons, or rounds

    _____ Ostinato

    _____ Unaccompanied singing

2. Villa-Lobos' *Bachianas Brasileiras* were influenced by: (411)
    a. the music of J. S. Bach
    b. the folk music of Brazil
    c. Stravinsky's early ballets
    d. Richard Wagner's music dramas
    e. (a) and (b), but not (c) and (d)

3. Contrast Puccini's *La Bohème* with Menotti's *The Medium.* (328-333
    and 416-418)

	La Bohème	The Medium
Full orchestra without piano		
Small orchestra with piano		
Over one hour long		
Less than one hour long		
Several stage settings		
Only one stage setting		
Has no chorus part		
Has a chorus part		
Verismo story		
Psychological story		

(continued)

64

4. The French composers following World War I, especially Erik Satie, were: (420)
   a. anti-romantic
   b. anti-German
   c. anti-modernistic
   d. opposed to composed music
   e. against vocal music

5. The French composer Darius Milhaud was influenced by: (420)
   a. jazz
   b. English folk songs
   c. Oriental music
   d. American Indian music
   e. Spanish-Gypsy music

6. Berg's opera *Wozzeck* follows a carefully designed scheme in terms of the music used for its 15 scenes (True or false). (412-413)

Listening Practice 13

Form

Listen to longer portions of music and then determine whether or not a melody or theme returns after another theme or musical section has been presented. Two consecutive appearances of a theme should not affect your answer; consider "theme return" as occurring only after the appearance of different musical material.

	Theme returns	Theme does not return
1. Franck—Violin Sonata, fourth movement		
2. Schubert—"The Erl King"		
3. Bernstein—"Quintet" from *West Side Story*		
4. Palestrina—*Sicut Cervus*		
5. Hindemith—*Kleine Kammermusik*, Op. 24 No. 2, fifth movement		
6. Beethoven—Symphony No. 5, first movement		

(Answers on page 85)

Study Exercise 29

Expressionism and Primitivism

1. What are the characteristics of expressionism?   (422-423)

2. A leading expressionistic composer was: (423)
    a.   Claude Monet
    b.   Arnold Schoenberg
    c.   Maurice Ravel
    d.   Jean Sibelius
    e.   Igor Stravinsky

3. Check the statements that are true about Arnold Schoenberg's *Pierrot Lunaire*.   (423-425)

    _____ It is an opera.

    _____ It is for full orchestra.

    _____ It is about a heroic man named Pierrot.

    _____ It is a good example of primitivism.

    _____ It contains many beautiful melodies.

4. *Sprechstimme* is: (423)
    a.   a type of rhythmic pattern
    b.   the German for *bel canto*
    c.   a half-spoken, half-sung style of singing containing no specific pitches
    d.   an opera by Arnold Schoenberg
    e.   the German word for "expressionistic"

5. Primitivism was an interest in the art and music of non-Western and nonliterate civilizations.   (True or False)   (425)

6. Stravinsky's *The Rite of Spring* was originally: (425)
    a.   an opera
    b.   a chamber work
    c.   an art song
    d.   a ballet
    e.   a film score

(continued)

7. *The Rite of Spring* includes: (425-426)
    a. bitonality
    b. mixed meters
    c. careful directions to the instrumentalists
    d. unusual orchestral timbres
    e. all of the above

Study Exercise 30

Neoclassicism and Serialism

1. What does the term "Neoclassicism" refer to? (433-436)

2. Check the characteristics that are true of Neoclassical musical
    works. (433-437)

    _____ Use a large orchestra

    _____ Are short in length

    _____ Have passionate warm melodies

    _____ Contain sizable amounts of improvisation

    _____ Often contain counterpoint

3. A tone row contains all _____ tones in the chromatic scale.
    It (does/does not) have a tonal center. (441-442)

4. Match the term in the right-hand column with the definition in the
    left-hand column. (441)

    _____ The row backwards.   Inversion

    _____ The row upside down and   Retrograde
                          backwards.

    _____ The row upside down.   Retrograde-inversion

5. In addition to the tone row, Schoenberg and his followers displayed
    unusual attention to: (444)
    a. harmony
    b. timbre
    c. rhythm
    d. dynamics
    e. formal patterns

6. Webern's music is marked by: (446)
    a. long, massive works
    b. much use of percussion
    c. an economy in the use of sounds
    d. blatant, expressionistic dissonances
    e. the use of folksongs

(continued)

7. Compare the music of the twentieth century with that of the Romantic period by checking the characteristics that are true for each period.

	Romantic	Twentieth Century
Homophony predominates		
Some atonal music		
Some very dissonant chords		
Mixed meters		
Some "angular" melodies		
Much exploitation of rhythm		
Aleatory and serial music		
Rich, warm tibres		
Piano very important		
Some use of Baroque forms		

Listening Practice 14

Romantic and Twentieth-Century Music Compared

Compare the fifth movement of Hindemith's *Kleine Kammermusik* with Franck's Violin Sonata, fourth movement. You can put an "H" on the line for your response on Hindemith's music and an "F" for your response on Franck's.

1. Size of performing group

   Solo or small group _____ Large group

2. Melody

   Melodies not prominent _____ Melodies very prominent

   Narrow pitch range _____ Wide pitch range

   Smooth, songlike, continuously flowing _____ Short and fragmented

   No repeated phrases _____ Many repeated phrases

   Plain and unadorned _____ Highly ornamented

   Traditional scale patterns _____ Much nontraditional or chromatic alteration of pitches

3. Rhythm

   Regular metrical pattern _____ Irregular metrical pattern

   Simple rhythmic structure _____ Complex rhythmic structure

   Little or no syncopation _____ Much syncopation

4. Harmony and counterpoint

   Contrapuntal- polyphonic ___ Some sections contrapuntal; some homophonic ___ Homophonic

   Little imitation _____ Much imitation

   Generally consonant chords and intervals _____ Many dissonant chords and intervals

5. Loudness

   Few changes of loudness level _____ Many changes of loudness level

   Sudden, abrupt loudness changes _____ Smooth, gradual loudness changes

6. Timbre

   Consistent _____ Many wide changes

(continued)

7. Form

    Short _____ Long

    Little repetition of material _____ Much repetition of material

    Indicate any formal pattern with letters

Art Music since 1945

1. What type of music was created in the twentieth century by the advocates of strict control over a musical composition? (449-450)

2. What type of music was created by advocates of few controls over musical works? (450)

3. Microtonal music has enjoyed wide acceptance among twentieth-century musicians. (True or False) (451-452)

4. A "prepared piano" is one that has: (453)
    a. been especially tuned
    b. had tacks, coins, tape, and so on, put in it to change its timbre
    c. had its pedals disconnected
    d. its sounds electronically amplified
    e. a mechanism for playing chords by depressing only one key

5. *Musique concrète* is music that is made by: (454)
    a. natural objects—dried gourds and the like
    b. tape manipulation of natural sounds
    c. tape manipulation of the sounds of metal instruments
    d. taping of sounds made by a synthesizer
    e. taped sounds developed from a computer program

6. Electronic compositions are *not* played by performers. (True or False) (455-456)

7. An eclectic composer is one who: (458)
    a. writes electronic compositions
    b. uses what he considers the beat of each style
    c. uses tone-row and conventional harmony
    d. transcribes conventional works for electronic instruments
    e. utilizes the techniques of chance music

8. Check the compositional techniques and performers found in George Crumb's *Night of the Four Moons*: (459-463)

    _____ Tone rows

    _____ Strict metrical patterns

(continued)

_____ Much attention to timbres

_____ Small number of performers

_____ Sonata form

_____ Contains directions for stage placement and lighting

_____ Narrator

9. What is the main feature of chance music? (430-431)

10. To what type of philosophy is aleatory music related? (430-431)

Study Exercise 32

American Music before World War I

1. The most sophisticated music written in America before the Revolutionary War was from a community of people called: (468)
   a. Puritans
   b. Bretheran
   c. Moravians
   d. Menonites
   e. Amsterdamers

2. The most significant American composer at the time of George Washington was: (468-469)
   a. Francis Hopkinson
   b. John Frederick Peter
   c. William Billings
   d. Lowell Mason
   e. Francis Scott Key

3. The music for "Yankee Doodle," "America," and "The Star-Spangled Banner" is not originally American. (True or False) (470)

4. Theodore Thomas is important in the development of American music because: (474-475)
   a. He wrote compositions based on American folksongs.
   b. He brought outstanding performers from Europe to America.
   c. He laid the foundation for the symphony orchestras of today.
   d. He was the first outstanding American concert pianist.
   e. Through his magazine, he promoted American music.

5. One of the first American composers to be influenced by native American music was: (475)
   a. Louis Moreau Gottschalk
   b. Edward MacDowell
   c. Lowell Mason
   d. Stephen Foster
   e. Horatio Parker

6. Two American "impressionistic" composers were _____ and _____. (475-476)

7. At about the turn of the twentieth century Charles Ives was composing music that called for: (458)
   a. polytonality
   b. polyrhythm
   c. "sing-song" singing
   d. dissonant counterpoint
   e. all of the above

American Music in the Twentieth Century

1. Aaron Copland's *Appalachian Spring* was written as: (479)
   a. a ballet
   b. an opera
   c. a tone poem
   d. a film
   e. an oratorio

2. In what ways does George Gershwin's *Porgy and Bess* differ from
   traditional operas (those presented earlier in the book, for
   example)?   (482-483)

3. Elliott Carter's music is: (486)
   a. serial
   b. neoromantic
   c. neoclassical
   d. very nationalistic
   e. folk-like

4. Match the American composer to the appropriate fact about his life
   and work. (489-491)

   _____   First black composer to   Valdimir Ussachevsky
                       achieve international
                       recognition.

   _____   Neo-Romantic composer   Gunther Schuller
                       who was a leading
                       educator.

   _____   Educator and Director of   John Cage
                       Lincoln Center; wrote
                       work on themes of
                       Billings.

   _____   Composed some works con-   William Schuman
                       taining improvised jazz.

   _____   One of the two composers   William Grant Still
                       who founded electronic
                       music center.

   _____   Most experimental   Howard Hanson
                       American composer--
                       prepared piano, chance
                       music, etc.

5. What characteristic does the music of both Edgard Varese and Earle
   Brown have in common?   (490)

Twentieth-Century Composers Study Exercise

Bela Bartok   Paul Hindemith   Arnold Schoenberg
Benjamin Britten   Charles Ives   Igor Stravinsky
John Cage   Sergei Prokofiev   Heitor Villa-Lobos
George Gershwin   Erik Satie   Anton Webern

1. _____ One of the most important composers of this century; changed from primitivism to Neoclassicism.

2. _____ Russian composer who wrote well in all forms; works are often quite romantic in sound.

3. _____ One of the founders of the French anti-romantic movement.

4. _____ American composer who is noted for his experimental and chance music.

5. _____ German composer who was Neoclassical; promoted the idea of "useful" music.

6. _____ Austrian who was a romanticist early in his career, but then wrote expressionistic music, and later developed tone-row music.

7. _____ Innovative American composer who at the turn of this century was using many new techniques in his music.

8. _____ Austrian composer noted for his extremely intellectual serial music.

9. _____ A prolific Brazilian composer who was influenced by Bach and the folk music of his native land.

10. _____ American composer who was strongly influenced by jazz.

(continued)

11. _____ Hungarian composer who died in the United
States; especially known for piano music and
strong quartets, plus collections of folk
music.

12. _____ English composer who was especially strong at
writing operas.

Study Exercise 34

Jazz

1. What are some of the types of music that influenced jazz? (492)

2. Blues and ragtime preceded jazz. (True or False) (492)

3. What is a "blue note?" (493)

4. Check the characteristics that are found in traditional jazz. (493-496)

   _____ Much improvisation

   _____ Much syncopation

   _____ Complex harmony

   _____ Many pentatonic melodies

   _____ Sung with a breathy tone and vibrato

   _____ Intricate form

5. Match the type of jazz in the right-hand column with the characteristic in the left-hand column. (496-501)

   _____ Ostinato bass; pianist improvises   Dixieland
                    melodic figures in right-hand
                    part

   _____ Small groups play it; nearly con-   Boogie woogie
                    tinuous syncopation; dissonant
                    chords

   _____ Virtually no preconceived structure;   Swing
                    no harmonic pattern followed

   _____ Played by big bands; arrangements   Bop
                    important; often performed in large
                    dance halls

   _____ Contains two beats per measure; simul- Free form
                    taneous improvisation; popular in
                    the 1920s; tends to be loud and fast

Rock, Country, Soul, and Musical Theater

1. What types of music are generally considered to have been the predecessors of rock?   (502)

2. List seven characteristics of rock music.   (503-506)

    a. _____

    b. _____

    c. _____

    d. _____

    e. _____

    f. _____

    g. _____

3. Why is the recording technician important to the successful of most rock works?   (506)

4. What is the main audience for country-western music? For rhythm-and-blues?   (506-507)

5. What are some of the characteristics of soul music?   (507-509)

(continued)

6. How has the character of the Broadway musical changed over the years?
   (509-512)

Study Exercise 36

The Notation of Music

1. Name these notes.
    (516)

2. Draw a picture of 12 or 13 keys on a keyboard. Mark these pitches on
    it: F , A , D. (517)

3. Match the correct rest or note with its name. (513)

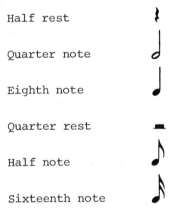

Half rest

Quarter note

Eighth note

Quarter rest

Half note

Sixteenth note

4. The top number of most meter signatures tells (the number of beats in
    a measure/which note value lasts for one beat). (514-515)

5. What are the differences in the arrangement of whole and half steps
    between major and minor scales? (518, 520)

6. A chord built on the fifth degree of a scale is called the (tonic/
    dominant) chord. (522)

(continued)

7. Parallel minor and major keys have: (522)
   a. the same key signature
   b. the same tonal center
   c. the same arrangement of whole and half steps
   d. the same meter signature
   e. both the same key signature and tonal center

Answers to Selected Listening Practices

Below are the answers to the Listening Pages dealing with the various elements of music. The pages in which two works are compared cannot be answered as precisely, and therefore are not included here.

Practice 1, Tempo: Wagner's Siegfried's Rhine Journey is slow; the Handel, Franck, and Carter works are moderate in tempo; Mozart's Piano Concerto No. 21, third movement, and Bartok's Concerto for Orchestra, fifth movement, are fast.

Of the three works, the Haydn Quartet is '1,' the Berlioz work is '2,' and the Hindemith Quintet is '3.'

Practice 2, Meter: The Brahms, Britten, and Mozart works are in three-beat meter; the other are in two- or four-beat meter.

Practice 3, Loudness: Bernstein's "Dance at the Gym," Brahms' Symphony No. 4, and Beethoven's Symphony No. 5 are loud; and others are soft.

Subotnik's Until Spring, Beethoven's Symphyny No. 5, and Mussorgsky's Boris Godunov change the level of loudness significantly; the others are rather steady.

Practice 4, Regular Meter: The Bernstein, Hindemith, and Crumb works have an irregular metrical pattern; the others do not.

Practice 6, Melodic Contour: The works by Franck, Morley, and Ives move to adjacent pitches; the other move about more.

Melodic Style: The works by Gershwin, Bach, and Villa-Lobos are smooth in style; the other are not.

Practice 8, Major/Minor: The works by Borodin, Mozart, and Handel are in major; the works by Brahms, Schubert, and Prokofiev are in minor; the work by Schoenberg has no tonal center.

Practice 9, Timbre: The works by Britten, Copland, Gabrieli, Berlioz, and Crumb have much change in timbre; the others do not.

Practice 10, Melodic Phrases: The works by Villa-Lobos and Puccini have flowing, continuous melodic lines; the others are much more separated.

Practice 13, Form: The theme returns in the works by Branck, Bernstein, Hindemith, and Beethoven; it does not in the Palestrina and Schubert works.

SCORES

Johann Sebastian Bach	Cantata No. 140, Part IV
Wolgang Amadeus Mozart	Symphony No. 40 in G Minor, First Movement
Wolgang Amadeus Mozart	Symphony No. 40 in G Minor, Third Movement
Franz Joseph Haydn	String Quartet, Op. 76 No. 3, Second Movement
Giacomo Puccini	*La Boheme*, Act I (libretto-score excerpt)
Johannes Brahms	Symphony No. 4 in E Minor, Op. 98, Fourth Movement
Modest Mussorgsky	*Boris Godunov*, "Coronation Scene"
Claude Debussy	*Prelude to the Afternoon of a Faun*

CANTATA NO. 140
Part IV

Johann Sebastian Bach

auf.
forth.

Ihr Freund kommt vom Him - mel präch - - tig,
Her Friend comes from Heav'n in splen - dor,

von Gna - den stark, von Wahr - heit mäch - - -
in mer - cy strong, in truth al - might - - -

Ho - si - an - na!
Sing Ho - san - na!

Wir fol - gen
We fol - low

All' zum Freu - den - saal,
all   to fes - tive hall,

und hal - ten mit das A - bend - mahl.
and share in our Lord's Sup - per there.

SYMPHONY NO. 40 IN G MINOR, K. 550
First Movement

Wolfgang Amadeus Mozart

SYMPHONY NO. 40 IN G MINOR, K. 550
Third Movement

Wolfgang Amadeus Mozart

Full orchestra

p Flute

40

TRIO (Section B): Theme a

Fine

p Strings

Oboe

50 Flute

p

Bassoon

Flute

f

p

60

Violins

Theme b

Low strings   Woodwinds   Low strings   Woodwinds   Low strings   Wood-winds

Theme a

70

Horns, Strings

Horns

cresc.　　　　　　*f* Flute　　　　　　　　　　　　*p*

Violins　　　　　　　　　　with Flute

Menuetto D.C.

After repeat , return
to begin·ning of minuet.

STRING QUARTET, OP. 76 NO. 3
Second Movement

Franz Joseph Haydn

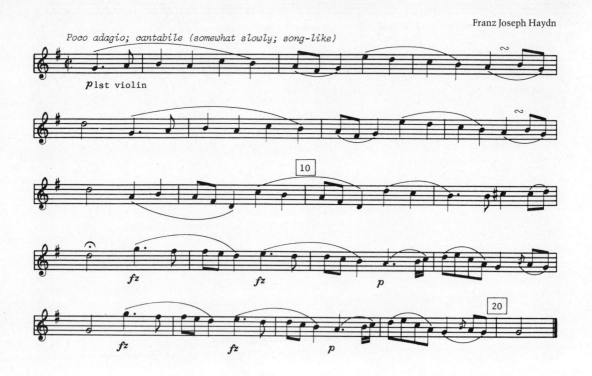

Var. II
1st violin
Cello

Var. III

2nd violin

70

1st violin

80

Var. IV

1st violin

8va - - - - - - - - - - - - - - -

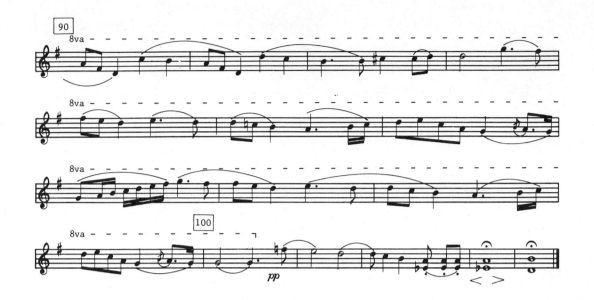

LA BOHÈME

GIACOMO PUCCINI (1858–1924)

Rodolfo:
Non sono in vena.

Rodolfo:
I'm just not with it.

(A timid knock is heard at the door.)

Chi è là?

Who's there?

Mimi:
Scusi.

Mimi:
Excuse me.

Rodolfo:
Una donna!

Rodolfo:
It's a lady!

Mimi:
Di grazia, mi s'è spento il lume.

Mimi:
Forgive me, sir, my candle's gone out.

Rodolfo: (opening the door)
Ecco.

Rodolfo: (opening the door)
There now.

Mimi:
Vorrebbe? . . .

Mimi:
If you could? . . .

Rodolfo:
S'accomodi un momento.

Rodolfo:
Please stay for just a moment.

Mimi:
Non occorre.

Mimi:
No, don't bother.

Rodolfo:
La prego, entri.

Rodolfo:
I beg you, come in.

(Mimi enters, but is seized with a fit of coughing.)

Rodolfo:
Si sente male?

Rodolfo:
You're feeling ill?

Mimi:
No . . . nulla.

Mimi:
No . . . nothing.

Rodolfo:
Impallidisce!

Mimi:
Il respir . . . Quelle scale . . .

(She becomes faint. Rodolfo supports her and helps her to a chair.
The candlestick and a key drop from her hand.)

Rodolfo:
Ed ora come faccio? Così!

(He gets some water and sprinkles it on her face.)

Che viso d'ammalata!

(Mimi revives.)

Si sente meglio?

Mimi:
Sì.

Rodolfo:
Qui c'è tanto freddo.
Segga vicino al fuoco . . . Aspetti . . .
un po' di vino . . .

Mimi:
Grazie.

Rodolfo: (pouring a glass)
A lei.

Mimi:
Poco, poco.

Rodolfo:
Così?

Mimi:
Grazie.

Rodolfo: (to himself)
Che bella bambina!

(Mimi sees the candlestick that she dropped when she became faint.)

Mimi:
Ora permetta che accenda il lume.
È tutto passato.

Rodolfo:
Tanta fretta?

Rodolfo:
You're turning quite pale!

Mimi:
I can't breathe . . . It's the stairway . . .

Rodolfo:
What can I do to help her? I know!

How very pale her face is!

Do you feel better?

Mimi:
Yes.

Rodolfo:
It is very cold here.
Sit nearer to the fire . . . One moment . . .
a little wine now . . .

Mimi:
Thank you.

Rodolfo: (pouring a glass)
For you.

Mimi:
Just a little.

Rodolfo:
Like this?

Mimi:
Thank you.

Rodolfo: (to himself)
A lovely young woman!

Mimi:
Now may I ask you to light my candle.
I feel much better.

Rodolfo:
What, so quickly?

109

Mimi:
Sì.

Mimi:
Yes.

(Rodolfo picks the candle up off the floor and lights it for her.)

Grazie.
Buona sera.

Thank you.
A good evening.

Rodolfo:
Buona sera.

Rodolfo:
A good evening.

(Mimi leaves and Rodolfo returns to his table.)

Mimi: (outside but reentering, she stops on the threshold of the door, which is open)

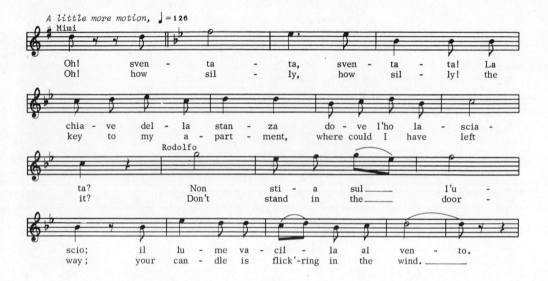

A *little more motion,* ♩ =126

Mimi
Oh! sven - ta - ta, sven - ta - ta! La
Oh! how sil - ly, how sil - ly! the

chia - ve del - la stan - za do - ve l'ho la - scia -
key to my a - part - ment, where could I have left

Rodolfo
ta? Non sti - a sul l'u -
it? Don't stand in the door -

scio; il lu - me va - cil - la al ven - to.
way; your can - dle is flick'-ring in the wind.

(Mimi's candle goes out.)

Mimi:
Oh Dio! Torni ad accenderlo.

Mimi:
Good heavens! Please light it once again.

(Rodolfo runs across the room with his candle.
As he nears the door his light is also blown out. The room is dark.)

Rodolfo:
Oh Dio! Anche il mio s'è spento!

Rodolfo:
Oh God! Now mine's gone out also!

Mimi:
Ah! e la chiave ove sarà?

Mimi:
Oh! and my key, where can it be?

(Groping about, she puts her candle on the table.
Rodolfo finds himself near the door and fastens it.)

Rodolfo:
Buio pesto!

Rodolfo:
Cursed darkness!

Mimi:
Disgraziata!

Mimi:
I've brought bad luck!

Rodolfo:
Ove sarà?

Rodolfo:
Where can it be?

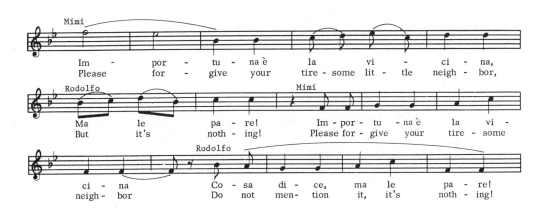

Im - por - tu - na è la vi - ci - na,
Please for - give your tire - some lit - tle neigh - bor,

Ma le pa - re! Im - por - tu - na è la vi -
But it's noth - ing! Please for - give your tire - some

ci - na Co - sa di - ce, ma le pa - re!
neigh - bor Do not men - tion it, it's noth - ing!

Mimi:
Cerchi.

Mimi:
Look for it.

Rodolfo:
Cerco.

Rodolfo:
I am.

(Rodolfo puts down his candle and searches for the key with his hands on the floor.)

Mimi:
Ove sarà?

Mimi:
Where can it be?

Rodolfo:
Ah!

Rodolfo:
Ah!

(He finds the key, but quickly slips it in his pocket.)

Mimi:
L'ha trovata?

Mimi:
Have you found it?

Rodolfo:
No!

Rodolfo:
No!

Mimi:
Mi parve . . .

Mimi:
It seemed that . . .

111

Rodolfo:
in verità!

Rodolfo:
I thought I had!

Mimi:
Cerca?

Mimi:
Looking?

(Pretending to search, Rodolfo works toward Mimi's voice.)

Rodolfo:
Cerco!

Rodolfo:
Looking!

(As they search along the floor, their hands meet.)

Mimi: (surprised)
Ah!

Mimi: (surprised)
Oh!

(Rodolfo holds on to Mimi's hand.)

♩ = 58

Rodolfo *gently*

Che ge - li - da ma - ni - na, se la la - sci ris - cal -
Your ti - ny hand is fro - zen; let me warm it in my

dar. Cer - car che gio - va? Al bu - io non si
own. Our search, why both - er? It's much too dark to

Harp

10

tro - va.
find it.

Ma per for - tu - na è una not - te di lu - na,_____
But soon the light of the moon will_____ help us,_____

slower

e qui la lu - na l'ab - bia - mo vi -
_____ and in the moon - light we'll look by the

20

Original tempo

ci - na. A - spet - ti si - gno - ri - na, le di -
win - dow. So lis - ten, pret - ty maid - en, while I

112

ro con due pa - ro - le chi son, chi son,
tell you in a few words just who I am,

e che fac - cio, co - me___ vi - vo.
what I do and how___ I ___ live.

slower   *Andante*
Vuo - le? chi son,___ chi son? Sono un po -
Shall I? I am,___ I am? I am a

e - ta. Che co-sa fac - cio? Scri - vo. E co - me
po - et. What is my work?___ Writ - ing. Is it a

vi - vo? Vi - vo. In po - ver -tà mia
liv - ing? Bare - ly. In po - ver -ty I

lie - ta scia - lo da gran si - gno - re___ rime ed in - ni d'a -
glad - ly la - vish on lone - ly lad - ies___ rhymes and hymns of af -

mo - re. Per so - gni e per chi - me - re e per cas - telli in
fec - tion. In dreams and flights of fan - cy and cas - tles in the

a - ria___ l'a - nima ho mi - lio - na
air___ tru - ly I am a mil - lion -

with expression
ria. Ta - lor dal mio for - zie - re ru - ban tutti i gio -
aire. Now all of those po - ses - sions have been sto - len like

ie l - li due la - dri: gli oc-chi bel - li. V'en -
jew - els by two thieves: your eyes so love - ly. You've

trar con voi pur o - ra, ed i miei so - gni u-sa - ti
been here just a short time, but all my u - sual day-dreams

Slower
e i bei so - gni mie - i _____ to - sto si di - le -
and all my oth - er fan - cies _____ now they have dis - ap -

Much slower *Original tempo* 60
guar! _____ Ma il fur - to non m'ac - co - ra
peared! _____ But still the theft can't grieve me

Slower
poi - chè, _____ poi - chè v'ha pre - so stan - za la dol - ce spe -
be - cause, _____ be - cause here at last sweet hope has seized my heart and

ran - za! _____ Or che mi co - no - sce - te
be - ing! _____ Now that you know a - bout me,

quicker *slower*
par - la - te vo - i, deh! par - la - te, chi sie - te?
please tell me your tale; won't you tell me who you are?

Mimi 70 *with simplicity*
p
Vi piac - cia dir! _____ Sì. Mi
Please say_ you will! _____ Yes. They

Andante-slowly
chia - ma - no Mi - mi ma il mio no - me è Lu - ci - a _____
call_ me Mi - mi, but my name is Lu - ci - a _____

114

La sto - ria mia è bre - ve,_____ A te - la oa
My sto - ry is a short one,_____ I do em -

se - ta ri - camo in ca - sae fuo - ri. Son tran - quil - la e
broid - 'ry on silk, in - doors and out - side. I'm con - tent and

Slower

lie - ta ed è mio sva - go far gi - gli e ro - se_____ Mi
hap - py; for lei - sure I make lil - ies and ros - es_____ I

Andante calmo

piac - cion quel - le co - se che han sì dol - ce ma -
real - ly love those flow - ers; they are sweet and de -

slower

li - a, che par - la - no d'a - mor, di pri - ma - ve - re,
light - ful; they speak to me of love, of love - ly spring - time,

che par - la - no di so - gni e di chi - me - re,_____ quel - le
they speak to me of fan - cies and il - lu - sions,_____ of such

return to tempo

co - se che han no - me po - e - si - a. Lei m'in -
plea - sures as on - ly po - ets know. Are you

Rodolfo   Mimi

ten - de? Sì. Mi chia - ma - no Mi -
list - 'ning? Yes. They call_____ me Mi -

Allegro moderato

mi, il per - chè non so. Sol - la, mi fo il
mi, but I don't know why. Liv - ing a - lone, I

115

pran - zo da me stes - sa. Non va - do sem - pre a mes - sa ma
eat a sim - ple din - ner. I sel - dom go to Mass, but

prego as - sai il Si - gnor. Vi - vo sol - la, so - let - ta,
oft - en pray to God. I'm a - lone and it's lone - ly,

là in u - na bian - ca ca - me - ret - ta:
up there in my one room a - part - ment;

guar - do sui tet - ti e in cie - lo,
look- ing at the house - tops and at the sky,

ma quan - do vien lo sge - lo il pri - mo so - le è
But when the frost is o - ver, sun - shine's first rays are

mi - o, il pri - mo ba - cio del - l'a -
mine, then comes the first sweet kiss of

pri - le è mi - o! il pri - mo so - le è
Ap - ril, to me! The first bright sun - shine is

mi - o! Ger - mog - lia in un va - so u - na ro - sa. Fog - lia a fog - lia la
mine! A rose starts to bud in its ves - sel. Leaf by leaf there it

spi - o! Co - sì gen - til il pro - fu - mo d'un fior
o - pens! How ten - der then is the scent of a flow - er

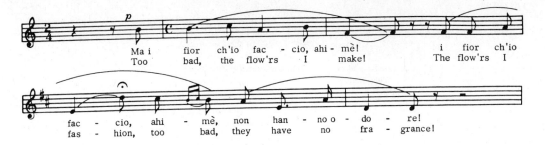

Ma i fior ch'io fac - cio, ahi - mè! i fior ch'io
Too bad, the flow'rs I make! The flow'rs I

fac - cio, ahi - mè, non han - no o - do - re!
fas - hion, too bad, they have no fra - grance!

Mimi:
> Altro di me non le saprei narrare:
> sono la sua vicina che la vien
> fuori d'ora a importunare.

Mimi:
> Other than that, there's not much more
> to tell you. I am merely a neighbor
> who intruded and came at a bad moment.

(Rudolfo's friends call from the courtyard to urge him to hurry to the Cafe.)

Schaunard:
> Ehi! Rodolfo!

Schaunard:
> Hey! Rudolfo!

Colline:
> Rodolfo!

Colline:
> Rodolfo!

Marcello:
> Olà. Non senti?

Marcello:
> Hey, you. You hear us?

(Rodolfo, though annoyed, goes to the window to answer.)

Marcello:
> Lumaca!

Marcello:
> You big snail!

Colline:
> Poetucolo!

Colline:
> Poet second-rate!

Schaunard:
> Accidenti al pigro?

Schaunard:
> Is the sluggard injured?

Rodolfo:
> Scrivo ancor tre righe a volo.

Rodolfo:
> I must write three lines all over.

Mimi:
> Chi son?

Mimi:
> Who're they?

Rodolfo: (turning to Mimi)
> Amici.

Rodolfo: (turning to Mimi)
> My colleagues.

Schaunard:
> Sentirai le tue.

Schaunard:
> You'll hear words from us.

Marcello:
> Che te ne fai lì solo?

Marcello:
> How can you stay alone there?

Rodolfo:
Non son solo. Siamo in due.
Andate da Momus, tenete il posto.
ci saremo tosto.

Rodolfo:
I'm not alone. Someone's with me.
Go on to Momus now, reserve a table.
We'll be there before long.

(Rodolfo watches at the window to make sure his friends go.
They gradually disappear from his sight.)

Marcello, Schaunard, Colline:
Momus, Momus, Momus,
zitti e discreti andiamocene via.
Momus, Momus!

Marcello, Schaunard, Colline:
Momus, Momus, Momus,
softly, discretely, we'll go off to eat.
Momus, Momus!

Marcello:
Trovò la poesia!

Marcello:
He's found true poetry!

Schaunard, Colline:
Momus, Momus, Momus!

Schaunard, Colline:
Momus, Momus, Momus!

(Rodolfo turns to see Mimi standing as if wreathed in the moonlight.)

118

119

gnor!   Che m'a - mi di',   Io t'a - mo!
sir!   Say you love me,   I love you!

A- mor,   a - mor!
My love, my love!

A - mor.
My love.

Orchestra

End of Act I

SYMPHONY NO. 4 IN E MINOR, OP. 98
Fourth Movement

Johannes Brahms

128

131

BORIS GODUNOV
("Coronation Scene")

Prologue, Scene 2

Modest Mussorgsky

ff Woodwinds, Strings (plucked), Glockenspiel

e - vil pre - sent - i - ments op - press my spir - it. O saint long dead,

O thou my roy - al fa - ther! Thou see'st in heav'n thy

faith - ful ser - vant's tears! Look down on

me and send a bless - ing from on high up - on my king - dom!

May I be true and mer - ci - ful, as thou, and jus - ti -

fy my peo - ple's praise,

Clarinets

p

Boris

Now let us go and kneel in prayer be - fore the tombs of Rus - sia's kings.

And then the peo - ple all shall feast. Come, ev' - ry

one from no - ble down to serf; all shall find room, all

find an hon - ored wel - come.

tr *Fast* *Sopranos*

sf Strings *ff* glo - ry!

Strings 10

glo - ry, glo - ry!

ff

PRELUDE TO THE AFTERNOON OF A FAUN

Claude Debussy